healing with
meditation

A concise guide to clearing, focusing and calming the mind

John Hudson

HH
HERMES
HOUSE

The edition published by Hermes House

© Anness Publishing Limited 2002 updated 2003..

Hermes House is an imprint of Anness Publishing Limited,
Hermes House, 88–89 Blackfriars Road, London SE1 8HA

Publisher: Joanna Lorenz
Production Controller: Joanna King

Publisher's Note:

The Reader should not regard the recommendations, ideas and techniques
expressed and described in this book as substitutes for the advice of a
qualified medical practitioner or other qualified professional.
Any use to which the recommendations, ideas and techniques
are put is at the reader's sole discretion and risk.

Printed in Hong Kong/China

3 5 7 9 10 8 6 4

contents

introduction

Meditation can help to bring the body and mind into a state of harmony, so that relationships with people are more fruitful, work flows more efficiently and problems are more easily solved. It is a way in which to balance an active life with calming periods of inner reflection.

This book introduces you to simple meditation techniques and offers you suggested ways in which to practise them. It provides guided meditations for specific purposes, such as those to help improve confidence and make important decisions. Whether at home, on a crowded train or in a busy office, you can reduce stress and bring yourself to a greater state of awareness and tranquillity through the power of meditation.

What is meditation?

People have always had the need to seek inner peace and relaxation, for spiritual and health reasons and self-realization. By practising just 20 minutes a day, you can achieve and enjoy the wonderful benefits of meditation.

Just what is meditation? Most simply put, it is sitting and relaxing. Many people find that their lives are so full of the demands of work, family, friends and organized leisure pursuits that they have no time to "stand and stare". Some are so caught up in planning and working towards the future that they take little pleasure from the here and now. In their bustle to "get on", they miss out on the simple pleasures of life: the changing seasons, birds singing or children discovering the beauty of life.

Beauty and joy, however, can be experienced in the most industrial of landscapes or the most difficult living situations. Meditation is a good way of taking time out and allowing yourself to tune into and appreciate the moment, whether you happen to be walking along the seashore, sitting by a stream, or just noticing and enjoying the intensity of silence in a still room.

▼ MEDITATION CAN HELP YOU TO REACH YOUR INNER RESPONSES TO THE WORLD AROUND YOU.

▲ Sit with your feet flat on the ground and your hands resting in your lap.

Getting comfortable

Rather than push yourself to adopt some strained physical position for meditation, just relax – sit in a chair or stroll through your favourite landscape at a steady pace. It is better not to slump or lie down when you are learning to meditate, as this could lull you into sleep: a state of relaxed attentiveness is what is desired. If you sit on a chair, do so with your feet flat on the floor, hands resting in your lap or on the arms of the chair, and your head comfortably balanced. If you are walking, take slow, careful steps – be aware of the movement of each foot, and its contact with the ground beneath.

Being here and now

Above all, meditation is about staying with the moment, about being in touch with your surroundings and your inner world. To experience this spirituality, you need not be a part of any organized religion. Although most religions do use some form of focused contemplation to promote spiritual awareness, meditation is also a technique that can be used for stress management or simply as a method to gain self-awareness.

Meditation is a pleasant way to gain deep relaxation, one in which you allow precious time for yourself. Simply meditating on a regular basis can be beneficial, but using words and images while practising can promote a marked improvement in your general wellbeing or in a specific area of life. It can even help you gain confidence when planning for upcoming events.

The benefits of meditation come from regular use. If under stress, you may find that meditating twice daily will restore composure and reduce irritability. It is best to allow at least ten, and ideally 20, minutes in meditation at each session.

A brief history of meditation

Meditation has been used throughout the world in all cultures. From informal reflection to the formal prayers held at retreats and on pilgrimages, meditation can lead us to a greater understanding and acceptance of ourselves and others.

In many people's minds, meditation is perhaps most closely linked with Buddhism – indeed, it was the main practice through which Buddhism's founder, Gautama, finally realized the state of enlightenment. Buddhism has defined many stages of meditation that are commonly practised for the purpose of achieving the ultimate level of purifying the mind and clearing away all thoughts and

mental images. Meditation is a kind of "emptying" of the mind of distracting thoughts and ideas.

THE PRACTICE OF YOGA
From the Hindu tradition, one of the best-known practices of meditation is yoga, the yoking or harnessing of mental and physical powers. Most of us think in terms of "hatha" or royal yoga, which is a series of physical exercises and postures performed to gain physical, and therefore mental, control. Less well known is "bhakti" yoga – a focusing of the mind, a style that is akin to the meditation outlined in this book; this is practised in Christian religions, as well. According to this

◄ A REPRESENTATION OF THE BUDDHA, WHICH FOLLOWERS USE AS A FOCUS FOR MEDITATION.

discipline, the practitioner sits and focuses his or her attention upon an aspect of their god. In doing so, they gain insights into their own responses

▲ MEDITATION IS A PART OF ALL THE WORLD'S RELIGIONS.

to the knowledge they have of that god's powers – the "god within" – and the lessons to be drawn from stories told of him or her.

CONTEMPLATIVE MEDITATION
It has long been a tradition in Christian religious communities, such as convents and monasteries, for monks and nuns to set aside a period of time each day to practise quiet contemplation. At such times, they often focus

on a crucifix and contemplate the passion of Christ, and all that it symbolizes for the believer. This is, of course, meditation, and it has all the benefits of helping the individual come to an understanding of his or her inner beliefs and response to their faith. In recent years, the practice has also become increasingly popular among many lay Christians.

◀ MIND AND BODY WORK TOGETHER IN MEDITATION TO PROMOTE HEALTH AND WELLBEING.

The mental & physical benefits

A potent physical and psychological therapy, meditation can be as strong as a commercial drug in helping the body and mind to keep illness and depression at bay. Practised regularly, it can promote a continued state of good health.

An individual emerging from a period of meditation, however brief, will notice a change in their emotional state from when they began the exercise. This can present itself in many ways, often as the sensation of being refreshed, with a more positive attitude and a general feeling of wellbeing. Situations and people that had been irritating and worrisome before may now be seen in a new and more positive way. The meditator may feel more in control, and less anxious.

These reactions have been known for years, but it is only in recent times that a physiological explanation has been available. Knowledge gained from brain scans and the measurement of brainwave patterns has given medical experts new information about the "alpha state" that results from meditation.

THE ALPHA STATE

When we are truly relaxed there are stages of change in the brainwave pattern, until it predominantly falls into the alpha state. Within this state, the brain triggers chemicals called endorphins – it is these substances that produce the feelings of wellbeing. Endorphins have even been called "nature's own opiates", and the good feelings that they induce can

◀ THE CHANGE IN BRAINWAVE PATTERNS CAUSED BY REGULAR MEDITATION CAN GIVE YOU A FEELING OF ALERT CALMNESS AND INCREASED MENTAL COMPOSURE.

◀ MEDITATING DURING TIMES OF STRESS MAY HELP YOU TO FEEL AS IF YOU ARE BACK IN CONTROL AGAIN.

continue for some time after the meditation has ended. The length of time will vary from one individual to another.

There is also a very real physical benefit: since these same endorphins also boost the immune system, they help the body to fight infection and disease, promoting a state of enduring good health.

Meditation for a busy work life

The pressures of modern life often mean that people are so busy, they maintain a level of constant activity throughout the day. Not only are they stifling their emotional responses, they are also pushing their health to the limit.

Many experts on stress management emphasize the need for a period of mental and physical relaxation at different stages during the day. They point out that by taking this time out, one actually gains rather than loses when it comes to productivity, as the brain simply cannot maintain intense activity for long periods and remain efficient.

THE 20-MINUTE RULE

Writer Ernest Rossi has formulated the "20-minute rule", which is based on the theory of ultradian rhythms. Ultradian rhythms are biorhythms that the body works through during each day – a little like hyperbolic curves of energy that repeat every 90 to 120 minutes or so. Naturally, it would be best to work only at peak performance times, but in lieu of this, timing your work breaks to coincide with the mind/body slow-down pattern every 90 minutes ensures maximum productivity and inhibits the build-up of stress.

▲ STRESS CAN BECOME DAMAGING WHEN WE ARE NO LONGER ABLE TO CONTROL OUR RESPONSES TO IT.

Rossi suggested a pattern of working for 90 minutes and then taking a 20-minute break, so as to completely change the mind/body state. Ideally, you should stop all work activity and experience a change of physical status (stand rather than sit, look into the distance rather than close up, for example) and mental focus. A 20-minute meditation is ideal, and you should be able to feel the benefits instantly.

TAKE A BREAK

Is it coincidence that workers throughout the world have evolved breaks at approximately 90-minute intervals (coffee, lunch, tea)? This has grown up through experience, and has occurred in all types of work environment. On returning to work after the break, you will view tasks and challenges afresh and be able to deal with

▲ MEDITATION HELPS YOU TO REMAIN CALM WHEN UNDER STRESS.

them more quickly and efficiently, as the mind and body are alert and ready to climb up to peak performance again on the biorhythmic curve. The feeling of wellbeing will continue well into the next 90-minute period.

Unfortunately, the intense demands of modern work practices, instant communication, and rising numbers of self-employed workers have meant that more people take their breaks at the desk, or ignore breaks altogether. This is a false economy, based on the premise that one can keep going indefinitely – in fact, it leads to greater inefficiency and is harmful to both the worker and their work.

◀ BE AWARE OF YOUR BIOLOGICAL CLOCK THROUGHOUT THE WORKING DAY AND TRY TO TAKE A BREAK EVERY 90 MINUTES.

Gaining the meditative state: exercises

The first rule in approaching the meditative state is to learn to relax completely. When you stop working, the tension that has built up in your mind and body remains, and this must be diffused before you can benefit from rest.

A programme of exercises will loosen contracted muscles and make you feel refreshed, revitalized and physically relaxed. As well as unwinding the stresses in your body, exercise has the added benefit of releasing mental tension, so it can be a helpful prelude to every meditation session.

If strains and tensions are allowed to build up in the body, they may lead to a variety of aches and pains, as well as increasing mental strain and diminishing co-ordination and efficiency. A single session of exercises

for relaxation will instantly refresh and calm you. Loosening your muscles will also make you aware of areas of tension in your body, so that you can give some attention to the causes: improving your posture and the way you sit at your desk, or changing the shoes you wear when you are constantly on your feet.

Relaxation reduces not only muscular tension, but also rates of respiration and digestion, blood pressure and heart rate. It also increases the efficiency of the internal organs and the immune system.

▶ RELAX IN A POSITION THAT IS COMFORTABLE FOR YOU.

While it is vital to relieve tension when you feel it building up into aching or stiffness, it is better to avoid such a build-up by incorporating relaxation exercises into your daily routine. Use them to stretch stiff muscles when you get up in the morning, or during a mid-morning or afternoon break from work. At bedtime, taking a few minutes to release tension in your neck, back and shoulders will aid sound, relaxing sleep. Training your body to relax fully will calm your mind and prepare it for the meditative state.

STANDING RELAXATION EXERCISES FOR NECK, BACK AND SHOULDERS

1 Stand upright with your arms stretched above your head. Rise up on your toes and stretch further still.

2 Drop forward, keeping your knees relaxed, and let your arms, head and shoulders hang heavy and loose for a while.

3 Shake your head and arms vigorously, then slowly return to a standing position. Repeat the exercise two or three times.

2 Drop forward, allowing your head and arms to relax completely. Return to the starting position and repeat the exercise, staying aware of the changing tensions in the muscles.

1 Sit upright in a firm, low-backed chair with your lower back supported and feet placed squarely on the floor, hip-width apart. Raise your arms above your head and stretch them upwards, feeling the pull in your upper body. Look upwards and hold the stretch for 20–30 seconds.

3 To stretch the back, link your hands together behind the chair, and lift your arms slightly. Lean back gradually, arching your back over the chair, hold for 10 seconds, then repeat.

The three "Ss" of meditation

When you begin to meditate, there are three things that you can focus on to make the process easier and more fluid. These will help you to "close off" the outside world and concentrate on the rich vastness of the inner world.

STILLNESS

Being able to sit relaxed and completely still is very important: it will enable you to drift into the state of awareness where your inner world can be reached and enjoyed. If you start to fidget or become aware that you are not comfortable, the stream of concentration will be broken. The ideal is to maintain stillness throughout the meditation.

SILENCE

Many people use personal stereos to try and block out the noise around them, but this can be very counterproductive: it is much better to meditate during a quiet time of day and learn to create inner silence. This will encourage your mind to see images and hear sounds coming from your inner self. The more you allow images and feelings to surface, the less you will be distracted. A teacher once said that when you can meditate on a busy railway platform, you will know you can really meditate.

▲ MEDITATION IS THE BEST GATEWAY TO INNER WISDOM; FIND TIME EVERY DAY TO INCREASE YOUR ABILITY.

SENSITIVITY

When you begin any new meditation technique, it is important to listen, watch and perceive whatever images, symbols, sounds and other sensations appear in your mind. These may be vague and fleeting at first, but by noticing and focusing on them, you will aid the whole process. You will become more still and quiet, and your overall awareness will become sharper – in meditation and, eventually, in the rest of your life.

Deep breathing

The power of proper breathing should not be underestimated – it oxygenates the blood, aiding thought processes and boosting physical energy. It also assists the flow of toxins out of the bloodstream, thus reducing the effects of stress.

▲ COUNT EACH BREATH FROM ONE TO TEN.

In meditation, your breath provides an ever-present and easily accessible focus on which to concentrate – you are always breathing. Many schools of meditation advocate using the breath in various ways, such as imagining that the breath originates at certain points in the body. The areas usually focused on are the "hara" just below the navel and the "tan tien", the heart in the centre of the chest. The crown of the head, the base of the spine and the soles of the feet may all be included in the awareness.

There are many ways of concentrating the mind in order to distract the inner "voice" that chatters incessantly, worrying and becoming obsessive about problems or people:

• Slowly count your breaths, from one to ten.

• Notice the physical changes at the nostrils and the abdomen, as your breath moves in and out.

• Notice the inner stillness as you change from exhalation to inhalation, from inhalation to exhalation.

• Conjure up an image that evokes a feeling of joy and serenity. This could be a beautiful natural scene with mountains or ocean waves, the sun's rays or a child. Breathe the image into your heart.

◀ IMAGINE EACH BREATH ORIGINATES AT THE HEART.

ALTERNATE NOSTRIL BREATHING

For most of us, breathing is a very mechanical act, but during times of stress we often get into the habit of breathing incorrectly. Practise these exercises to become aware of each breath and to help your breathing become more rhythmical and steady. You should stop the exercise immediately if you start to feel dizzy, and should never force your breath.

1 As a useful aid to meditation, concentrate all of your attention on regular, quiet breathing. This is physically calming and also helps to clear your mind of any intrusive thoughts. Place the first two fingers of one hand on your forehead, with thumb and ring finger reaching down on either side of your nose.

2 Relax your thumb and inhale through that open nostril; pinch it closed again, then release the finger to breathe out through the other nostril.

3 Breathe in on the same side, then close that nostril and breathe out on the other side. Continue to breathe slowly through alternate nostrils.

Postures for meditation

Meditation is a personal experience, but one that you need not practise in private. You can meditate almost anywhere – on the bus, in the park, or sitting at your desk – but it is important to find a position that feels comfortable for you.

When choosing a position in which to meditate, remember that you should feel relaxed without drifting off to sleep. In addition, you should be able to remain still for the period of meditation without experiencing any numbness or cramp in your limbs, as this would be distracting and counterproductive. Experiment with the following suggestions until you discover which position feels best for you.

SITTING ON YOUR HEELS
This posture is a good one for your back, as it keeps the spine straight. Your feet should be relaxed, with the toes pointing backwards. Rest your hands lightly on your lap. Put a cushion underneath your feet if you wish.

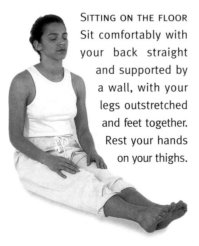

SITTING ON THE FLOOR
Sit comfortably with your back straight and supported by a wall, with your legs outstretched and feet together. Rest your hands on your thighs.

SITTING ON A CHAIR
Choose a firm chair that provides good support for your lower back. Put your feet together, resting them flat on the floor. Rest your hands on your thighs. Keep your back straight but relax your shoulders, and keep your head erect.

THE LOTUS POSITION

1 The half-lotus is the simpler version: bend one leg so that the foot rests under the opposite inner thigh. Place the second foot on top of the thigh of the first leg. Keep the spine upright, and rest the hands lightly on the knees.

2 To achieve the full lotus position, one leg should be bent with the foot resting on top of your other thigh; then bend your other leg so that the foot crosses over the first leg on to the opposite thigh.

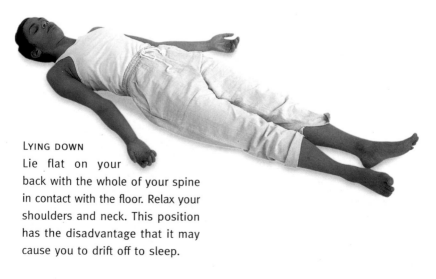

LYING DOWN
Lie flat on your back with the whole of your spine in contact with the floor. Relax your shoulders and neck. This position has the disadvantage that it may cause you to drift off to sleep.

Using sounds

Many adherents of transcendental meditation and religious groups talk of using a sound to assist with meditation. The repetition of a phrase, a word or a sound creates the alpha state by an almost hypnotic focus upon the sound.

An effortless sound, repeated with the natural rhythm of breathing, can have the same soothing, mentally liberating effect as the constant natural sound of running water, rustling leaves or a beating heart. The single sound, or mantra as it is known, is used to blot out the chatter of intrusive thoughts, allowing the mind to find repose.

Speaking or chanting a mantra as a stream of endless sound is a very ancient method of heightening an individual's awareness by concentrating the senses. The simple gentle sound "om" or "aum" is sometimes known as the first mantra, which is literally an instrument of thought. From the ancient Hindu language, the curving Sanskrit symbol for this primordial word represents the states of consciousness: waking, dreaming, deep dreamless sleep and the transcendental state.

The Hare Krishna movement is well known for its chant, which is repeated over and over again, and can lead its members to become "high" – again the effects of endorphin release. However, the sound need not be a special word or incantation; something simple and meaningful will be just as effective. Any word that appeals to you will do, repeated with the outflow of breath – silently in the mind, or spoken out loud.

▲ THE CONSTANT, YET VARIABLE SOUND OF RUNNING WATER CAN BE ESPECIALLY SOOTHING AND THERAPEUTIC.

Using touch

You can use your sense of touch in a soothing way to induce a state of meditation when you are under stress. Young children do this when they take a smooth ribbon or blanket end to hold and manipulate whenever they feel tense.

For centuries in the Middle East, people have benefited from the soothing sense of touch by using strings of worry beads: these are passed rhythmically through the fingers during times of stress and difficulty, in order to focus the mind and calm anxiety. The beads' uniform size, gentle round shapes, smooth surfaces and rhythmic, orderly clicking as they pass along their string all assist the state of mind.

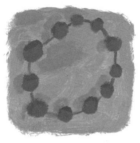

◀ FEEDING WORRY BEADS THROUGH YOUR FINGERS CAN HELP TO FOCUS AND CALM THE MIND.

You can use one or two smooth, rounded stones or crystals in the same way, passing them from one hand to the other, and concentrating on their temperature, shape and surface.

Alternatively, choose an object with a soothing and tactile quality that particularly appeals to you, such as a favourite velvet or silk scarf, which you can feed slowly from one hand to the other as you concentrate on clearing your mind.

▶ THE SMOOTH FEEL OF A SILK SCARF BETWEEN YOUR HANDS MAY HELP TO LULL YOU INTO THE MEDITATIVE STATE.

Using colours

Some colours are associated with relaxation. Summoning up and concentrating on these can be a helpful way to clear the mind of tension. They can be an ideal entry into the quiet of a meditation session.

Sit with your eyes closed, and be aware of the first colour that comes into your mind: it may be any colour of the rainbow – though red and purple are common. Slowly let the colour change to blue or green, allowing it to fill the whole of your mind's eye and replace all other colours; pink hues are also beneficial. A feeling of relaxation will grow as the new colour builds in your mind. When it is complete, you will experience pleasant feelings of inner peace and stillness.

BREATHING IN COLOUR

You can help the colour to build by associating it with your breathing. Establish a comfortable rhythm of breathing, and focus on it until your mind is clear. Allow the colour to fill your mind's eye; then, as you breathe in, imagine the colour filling your body, from the soles of your feet right up to the top of your head.

COLOUR VISUALIZATION EXERCISE

Shut your eyes and breathe calmly and regularly, focusing on your breathing. As you inhale, imagine that you are sitting on a soft lawn in a peaceful garden. Sense the cool freshness of the green surrounding you. As you exhale, imagine the silken magenta of a rose. Breathe in again and let the cleansing green fill your mind. Repeat this exercise once or twice, then sit quietly for a few moments.

▶ TRY TO BECOME AWARE OF THE WONDERFUL COLOURS OF THE NATURAL WORLD, SUCH AS IN THIS FIELD OF BRIGHTLY COLOURED TULIPS.

COLOUR PROPERTIES

lours are associated with various qualities, so choose a colour to suit your current
eds. Its complementary colour is shown in brackets. Often meditators visualize
)ving from their chosen colour to its complement – a way of creating change.
they may move from one colour to another to gain these qualities.

- Red: vitality, energy, strength and will power (turquoise)
- Orange: happiness and laughter (blue)
- Yellow: intellect and objectivity (violet)
- Green: cleansing and harmony (magenta)

- Turquoise: strengthens the immune system, counteracts disease (red)
- Blue: peace and relaxation, restful sleep (orange)
- Violet: beauty, dignity, self-respect (yellow)
- Magenta: release of obsessional thoughts and memories (green)

Using crystals

 Clear quartz has long been used as an aid to meditation. Gazing at a crystal can help you to focus – you are looking at solid matter, yet through it at the same time, and this can have an extraordinary effect on your ability to solve problems.

Sit quietly with a crystal for a few minutes to become sensitive to its energies – you will gain a greater insight as to how you can use it as a healing tool. Take time to look at your crystal in detail, then allow your focus to relax. Pay attention to your feelings and the quality of your thoughts. Are they calm or

▲ SIT COMFORTABLY AND GAZE INTO YOUR CHOSEN CRYSTAL.

hurried? Do they carry a particular memory or evoke a certain emotion? Notice any sensations in your body. After a minute or so, move on to the next crystal. Repeat the process and compare the experiences of the different stones.

To meditate with a chosen crystal, place or hold it at a comfortable distance on a table, so that you can easily gaze into the depths of the stone. Don't worry about your thoughts – just relax and gaze. Close your eyes for a few moments and take a couple of slow, deep breaths. Repeat the process several times, allowing your mind to clear itself of any clutter or

▲ SITTING QUIETLY WITH YOUR CRYSTALS ALLOWS YOU TO DEVELOP YOUR SENSITIVITY TO THEIR HEALING ENERGIES.

"chatter". Take a little time to return to normal activity when you finish the meditation.

If you find it difficult to settle down with one crystal, you can use your creative playfulness to arrange a mandala or other pattern with your stones. This form of active contemplation can be just as revealing and relaxing as "doing nothing". If you have room, make a large mandala of stones on the floor and spend time in its centre.

CALMING QUARTZ

Hold a smoky quartz in your left hand. Sit quietly with your eyes shut, or gaze gently into another crystal. After a few moments change the crystal around to the other hand. What differences do you feel? Once you find an effective combination, spend a few minutes each day sitting with your crystals.

▸ MAKE SURE THAT YOU ARE SITTING COMFORTABLY. PLACE YOUR CHOSEN CRYSTAL ON A TABLE, CLOSE YOUR EYES FOR A FEW MOMENTS TO HELP YOU RELAX AND THEN CONCENTRATE ON GAZING INTO THE STONE.

Using chakras

The subtle internal energy centres of the body are known as chakras. The chakras have been used for contemplation and spiritual development in both Eastern and Western cultures for thousands of years.

The seven classic chakras lie in a line through the centre of the body's trunk area, just in front of the spine and up into the head. They are usually treated in sequence from the lowest – the first or base chakra – upwards. Every time that you begin your meditation, try to visualize the position of each chakra in sequence. Over time, you will become more aware of the internal energies at these points.

▸ EACH CHAKRA HAS A PARTICULAR FOCUS OF ACTION BUT THEY ARE ALL INTERRELATED. WHEN ONE BECOMES DISTURBED IT CAN UPSET THE FUNCTIONING OF THE OTHER CHAKRAS.

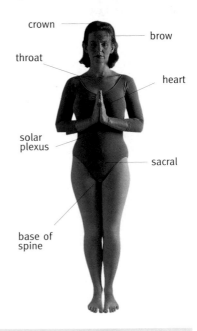

crown

brow

throat

heart

solar plexus

sacral

base of spine

CHAKRA PROPERTIES

chakra	positive qualities	negative qualities
1 base of spine	security, stability	primitive fears, survival
2 sacral (genitals)	sexual confidence, creativity	sexual weakness
3 solar plexus	personal power, self-worth	lack of confidence
4 heart	love, sense of freedom	emotional restriction
5 throat	self-expression	poor communication
6 brow	reliable intuition	lack of wisdom
7 crown	higher consciousness	material attachment

CHAKRA-BALANCING MEDITATION
The following exercise is a powerful way of activating and balancing personal energies, thus improving your overall health and wellbeing.

1 Sit comfortably, with your spine straight and relaxed. Breathe from your lower abdominal area and focus your attention on the first chakra, at the base of your spine. Imagine that you are breathing in and out of this point, and sense the external energies brought in by your breath.

2 Bring your attention to your second chakra, above the genitals, and repeat the process.

3 Continue the exercise through all the chakras, until you reach the crown chakra. You may find that with some of the chakras, the energies are a bit stagnant and a little extra time and attention is needed to bring them into focus.

4 Now review each chakra in turn, from bottom to top, and imagine you are unblocking the natural energy flow in each and redressing the balance between them.

5 Be aware that the base chakra connects you to the earth and the crown chakra to cosmic energies; sense the integration between your physical and spiritual energies with that of the whole universe.

◀ FOCUS ON THE CHAKRAS INDIVIDUALLY AND BREATHE IN AND OUT AT THE POINT OF EACH ONE.

meditation exercises

Once you have mastered the techniques for gaining the meditative state, you will be ready to progress to the next section. The following pages will introduce you to a number of guided programmes to help you on your way to an even deeper meditative state. You may find it helpful to record the exercises on tape, so that you can concentrate on gaining the images, or focusing attention, without worrying about forgetting a passage or having to refer to the appropriate page.

Once you are able to easily reach the deep meditative state you will be ready to tackle specific problem areas in your life by practising the relevant healing meditations.

The numbers game

This is a simple meditation that uses a blackboard – real or imaginary. It is a good "game" to use with children, to give them an experience of meditation. Practised after bath-time, it is an ideal way to relax in the evening.

The game is presented as if you are leading a group of children, but it can be easily used by an adult. It is an excellent way to clear the mind through concentration, imagination and patterns, all of which are wonderful ways of gaining a real experience of deep meditation.

1 Ask the participants to sit or lie down in a relaxed position. Once they have found a really comfortable position, tell them to remember it, and then ask them to sit up. Tell them they are going to return to their relaxed positions in just a few moments.

2 With chalk on the blackboard, draw a diagram of numbers, three lines by three columns, making sure that there are no mathematical links, like this:

3	1	5
8	6	9
4	7	2

▶ EVEN CHILDREN CAN ENJOY AND BENEFIT FROM MEDITATION EXERCISES.

3 Give the children one minute – be sure that they see you are timing it – to memorize this pattern in lines and columns. They will be working with this later in their mind's eye (the imaginary screen on the inside of the forehead).

4 Ask them to return to their relaxed position, with their eyes closed. Tell them to concentrate on the numbers and, if anything else comes into their mind, to recognize it and push it away (repeat this often during the session).

5 Rub out lines or columns of numbers, telling the children what you are doing and asking them to do the same in their mind's own diagram – do this slowly. Keep the pace of your speech slow, too. Give them time to adjust, and tell them what is left as a check, for example, "That leaves just four numbers." Continue until they reach the last number, and say "Really concentrate on that number." Then take a long pause.

6 Rub out the last number, saying "Now concentrate on what is left." Let them remain in silence until you notice a restlessness – this is often after three or more minutes.

7 Wake them gently, by speaking in a soft voice becoming louder with an instruction to "Sit up." Ask them what the last number was and for their reactions.

The haven

Once you have managed to achieve a state of complete physical relaxation and calm, allow your mind to enter a place that is special to you. Whether real or imaginary, you will be able to rest and feel good about yourself in this place.

▲ CLOSE YOUR EYES AND ALLOW YOUR MIND TO DRIFT OFF TO YOUR FAVOURITE REFUGE FOR PEACE AND RELAXATION.

Where is this special place? It may be lying in bed, in a warm bath, or a place that you visited when you were a child, in a quiet corner of a wood, or a secret room in a ruined castle, where you found yourself suddenly away from all other people. Perhaps it is a windswept beach, where pieces of driftwood wash up on the sand. Whether a real or an imaginary place, it is somewhere you really can relax, safe and secure.

Go to your special place . . . feel what made it appeal to you . . . what makes it special still . . . It belongs only to you, so you can think and do whatever you like here . . . In this safe, secure place no one and nothing can ever bother you. Allow yourself to realize that this is a haven, a unique haven of tranquillity and safety, where you will always feel able to relax completely . . .

Now you can allow your mind to drift . . . drift. Notice what kind of light shines through the

branches or the drifting clouds or in through the window . . . Is it bright or hazy or dim? . . . Does the temperature feel soothingly warm or refreshingly cool? . . . What sounds do you hear? Distant voices, or perhaps birds singing . . . Be aware of the colours that surround you . . . the shapes . . . and textures . . . the familiar objects that make that place special. You can just be there . . . whether sitting, lying or reclining, enjoying the sounds . . . the smells . . . the atmosphere . . .

▲ CONJURE UP A TIME AND PLACE, REAL OR IMAGINARY, TO ADOPT AS YOUR SPECIAL MEDITATIVE PLACE.

No one is asking anything of you here . . . no one expects anything of you . . . you do not need to do anything . . . you have no need to be anywhere . . . except here in this peaceful place, where everything is perfectly calm and you can truly let yourself . . . relax. Breathe in the quiet solitude and feel completely at one with your tranquil private place.

A guided visit to a country house

This meditation takes you on a tour of a beautiful, old, country estate. Imagine that you are visiting a sprawling stately home, on a warm summer's afternoon. Begin by standing at the top of the wide staircase that leads down into the entrance hall.

▲ PICTURE YOURSELF IN THE GROUNDS OF A STUNNING STATELY HOME.

As you look down across the entrance hall, you can just glimpse a gravel drive through the open doors opposite, and sunlight on the gravel. There is no one around to bother you as you stand poised to descend the staircase . . .

You slowly begin to ease down the steps, and now you are moving down the last ten steps to the hallway, relaxing more as each foot reaches the next step:

10 Taking one step down, relax and let go . . .

9 Taking the next step down, feel at ease . . .

8 Becoming even more relaxed . . . let go even more . . .

7 Drifting deeper . . . and deeper . . . and even deeper down still . . .

6 Becoming calmer . . . and calmer . . . even calmer still . . .

5 Continuing to relax . . .

4 Relaxing further, let go even more . . .

3 Sinking deeper, drifting further into this welcoming, relaxed state . . .

2 Enjoy these good feelings, feelings of inner peace . . .

1 Nearly all the way down, feeling very good . . . feeling beautifully relaxed . . . and **0**.

You are wandering across that hallway now, towards the open doors and the gardens beyond, soaking up the atmosphere of peace and permanence in this lovely old building. You wander out through the doors and down the stone steps . . . and find yourself standing on a wide gravel drive that leads from the lush green lawns . . . and the shrubs and trees, towards the entrance gates. Notice the different shades of green and brown against a clear, blue sky . . . You can feel the sun's warmth on your head and shoulders on this beautiful afternoon . . . There are flowerbeds with splashes of colour happily bobbing in the gentle breeze. And there's nobody else about . . . no one needing anything, no one wanting anything and

▼ WALK STEADILY DOWN THE PATH, AWARE OF ALL THE COLOURS, SCENTS AND SOUNDS.

nobody expecting anything from you . . . You can enjoy the serenity and solitude of this pleasant garden that has existed for centuries.

Further down the driveway, you notice an ornamental fish pond. You wander down, with nothing disturbing the stillness of the afternoon but the crunch of the gravel as it moves beneath your feet, and the occasional bird song from far away . . . You are wandering down towards the fish pond, soaking up the atmosphere of the myriad flowers and butterflies.

Eventually . . . eventually you find yourself standing close to the edge of the fish pond, looking down into the clear, cool, shallow water, just gazing at the fish . . . large ornamental goldfish of red and gold, black and silver, swimming so easily . . . gliding so effortlessly among the pondweed, in and out of shadows and around the lily pads. Sometimes they seem almost to disappear behind the weed and shadows . . . but always they reappear, their scales catching the sunlight: red, gold, silver, black . . .

And as you stare at the fish, your mind becomes even more deeply relaxed . . .

a guided visit to a country house **37**

The well

This continues from the previous visualization of the country house. It is intended to take you to even deeper levels of meditation. Alternatively, you can use it just on its own to focus the mind, using the clarity and depth of the water.

As you watch the fish, you notice that the centre of the pond is very, very deep. It could be the top of a disused well . . .

You take from your pocket a silver coin and, with great care, toss the coin so that it lands over the very centre of the pond . . . then watch as it swivels down through the water. The ripples drift out to the edges of the pond, but you just watch the coin as it drifts and sinks, deeper and deeper through that cool, clear water, twisting and turning . . . Sometimes it seems to disappear as it turns on edge; at other times a face of the coin catches the sunlight and flashes through the water . . . sinking, drifting deeper and deeper, twisting and turning as it makes its way down.

Finally, it comes to rest at the bottom of the well, lying on a cushion of soft mud, a silver coin in the still, clean water . . .

And you feel as still and undisturbed as the coin . . . as still and cool and motionless as the water, enjoying the feeling of inner peace and utter tranquillity.

▾ WATCH THE SPREADING RIPPLES AS THE COIN LANDS IN THE CENTRE OF THE POND.

A mountain

Once you can reach a state of complete relaxation, you can use this time to focus your attention in various ways. You may meditate on an image to gain insights and self-knowledge. The mountain is a potent symbol for overcoming obstacles.

The mountain has existed for thousands of years . . . it stands tall . . . still . . . silent . . . and regal. Pushing up against the bright blue sky, nestled in-between the white, white clouds that drift past, its ancient ragged peak endures . . . for years . . . and centuries . . . and millennia. Nothing can shake the stillness of the mountain, its underlying rock made to last forever, its trees towering into the mist, their ever-changing cycles of life . . . beginning, ending, beginning again . . . Animals live among the trees and munch the plants tucked in the crevices . . . deer dwell here . . . birds nest up on the high rocks near the cliffs . . . and at the top of the mountain, at the very highest point, the air is crystal clear, imbued with the purest, invigorating oxygen . . . At the very highest point, the world stretches out before you, a vast tapestry of towns and lakes and continents . . . and as the sun sinks into the horizon, the infinite and uncountable stars glisten in a sky that stretches on forever . . . and forever . . . and forever.

▼ A MOUNTAIN MEDITATION HELPS YOU TO PUT PROBLEMS INTO PERSPECTIVE.

A flower

In this meditation, place a real flower in front of you. Use your chosen technique to obtain inner quiet. Now open your eyes and focus on the flower, a symbol of growth and rebirth. If you find thoughts or words developing, let them flow naturally.

Consider a single flower, in full bloom, the colour in the petals, the connection to the stalk, how each petal is formed, and the differences and similarities there. How natural and beautiful it is, the shading and subtle changes caused by the light . . . This flower is at its peak of perfection . . . soon the petals will open and then fall . . . a seed pod will develop there . . . the seeds will scatter . . . some will find earth in which to rest, and in the natural cycle of things will stay dormant . . . until the time is right . . . The light and temperature trigger new growth . . . a tiny shoot will develop and grow, emerging from the soil . . . larger leaves will unfold, then a stalk carrying a tiny green bud will emerge, and as this swells

◀ THE NATURAL CYCLE OF BIRTH, GROWTH, DEATH AND REBIRTH.

through the casing, the flower bud will appear . . . and form into another flower just like this one, and light and shade will allow its true beauty to be enjoyed again . . . Natural beauty . . . colour . . . light . . . shade . . . perpetual change . . . the seasons . . . death . . . decay . . . rebirth . . . growth . . . perfection . . . the natural cycle of living things.

▶ FOCUS YOUR MIND UPON A BEAUTIFUL, EXOTIC FLOWER IN FULL BLOOM.

A clock ticking

The hands of a clock record the passage of time: time never stands still, but our perception of it can change. Past – present – future, the clock registers the moments of life moving forward. Focusing on the image of a clock can be very therapeutic.

The clock ticks . . . the hands move . . . so slowly . . . always moving . . . seconds tick away . . . The one just past is over . . . a new second takes its place . . . it too is replaced . . . as time moves on. Each moment lasts for just a second . . . The clock may stop . . . time never stops . . . it moves on . . . and on . . . The moment that is over is out of reach . . . the moment to come has not yet arrived, but . . . this moment . . . is all MINE . . . this moment I can use exactly as I wish . . . I focus on this moment . . . I influence this moment . . . I can use this moment . . . and no other NOW!

Measurement . . . movement . . . monitoring . . . invention . . . mechanism . . . complexity . . . regularity . . . cogs . . . gears . . . chains . . . weights . . . pendulum . . . interaction . . . perpetual motion . . . never still . . . always moving . . . on and on . . . into the next moment . . . into infinity . . . for ever.

▼ YOU ARE ONLY ABLE TO INFLUENCE THE PRESENT MOMENT, SO TRY TO STAY FOCUSED ON THE HERE AND NOW.

A bird

This meditation is effective when you feel cares weighing you down, curtailing your freedom. It is even more effective when done outside in the fresh air. If you have the chance to watch a real bird, follow its flight as far as you can.

◄ PICTURE A COLOURFUL BIRD PERCHED ON TOP OF A TALL TREE.

it sang . . . soaring upwards and upwards . . . coasting through the serene blue sky . . . skimming the feather-light clouds so effortlessly. It doesn't have a care in the world . . . all its attention is concentrated on flying . . . swooping . . . swerving in and out of the clouds so gracefully . . . For the moment, it forgets about finding food for its mate and its chicks . . . for the moment, it is free to play . . . to glide . . . to sail through the huge swathe of azure, lost in the pure joy of flying . . . lost in the happiness of being alive . . .

A bird perches at the top of a tall tree . . . it sings . . . sings a song to its mate . . . sings a song to its chicks . . . Suddenly, it flutters its wings and takes off. Flying, it finds itself high above the tree in which

▲ FOLLOW THE FLIGHT AND MOVEMENTS OF A BIRD AS FAR AS YOUR EYE CAN SEE.

Healing meditations: for self worth

We all have attributes and qualities in which we can take pride and pleasure. This exercise is about emphasizing these positive aspects in order to allay the doubts that only serve to limit our potential; the exercise can enhance our enjoyment of life.

First, peruse the list of statements and fill in the sections in brackets; then begin the meditation.
• I like my [physical attribute]
• I am proud of my [attitude or achievement]
• I love meeting people – they are fascinating
• My contribution is valuable to [name person]
• I am lovable and can give love
• Others appreciate my [opinions, assistance, a personal quality]
• I enjoy being a unique combination of mind and body

Imagine yourself speaking to your colleagues, boss or friends . . . See yourself behaving and looking confident . . . Notice how you stand . . . hear the way that you speak . . . slowly, calmly, clearly, with confidence. You are communicating your needs . . . ideas . . . opinions in a positive way. Notice how your words flow easily, and how others listen attentively to you . . . valuing

▶ BE AWARE OF HOW YOU STAND, YOUR FACIAL EXPRESSIONS AND THE FEELINGS INVOLVED.

what you say. Now "climb aboard" – be there – get in touch with the stance . . . expression . . . feelings . . . and know that you can use these at any time to gain the inner strength that supports you in everything you do.

See yourself in different situations: at home, in a social setting, in all the spheres of your life, being a confident, self-assured person. You are valuing your own talents, and the inner strengths that come from experience . . . knowledge . . . skills . . . insights . . . understanding . . . attitudes . . . patterns of behaviour.

For cleansing the mind

 Meditating lets you focus on yourself with greater clarity. It allows you to sift through all your scattered energies, and release thoughts and desires you no longer need. Try this exercise to cleanse your psyche with healing rays of colour.

1 Close your eyes and imagine that you are sitting in a green meadow. A cool, crystal-clear stream runs nearby, with abundant fragrant flowers all around. It is a fine, bright day with a gentle breeze; the sky is blue, with a scattering of soft, white clouds.

2 Choose a colour that you need (see Colour Properties) for your personal healing and wellbeing.

3 Choose one of the clouds above you and fill it with the colour until it starts to shimmer with its sparkling light.

4 Let the cloud float over you. Allow it to release a coloured shower that envelops you with a sweet, sparkling mist, like stars cascading in all directions.

5 The mist settles on your skin and is gently absorbed, until it has completely saturated your system with its healing vibration.

6 Allow the hue to run through your bloodstream for 3–4 minutes, giving your body a therapeutic colour wash.

7 Let the pores of your skin open so that the coloured vapour can escape, taking any toxins with it. When the vapour runs clear, close your pores again.

8 Sit quietly with your cleared, healed body and mind for a few minutes. Take three deep breaths, releasing each gently, then open your eyes.

▸ MEDITATE OUT OF DOORS TO CONNECT TO YOUR HIGHER SPIRITUAL DIMENSION.

For maintaining stamina

In this meditation, you will use the enlivening colour gold to recharge your body and mind, letting its warmth restore your physical energy and lift your spirits. It is perfect for use in the midst of an active period, to help restore or maintain stamina.

1 Recline in a comfortable position and take a deep breath in. When you inhale, imagine yourself lying on a floating sunbed on the ocean or in a swimming pool, gently moving with the waves of the water.

2 Look up at the sky – it is pale blue, with an arch of pure gold, high up. Focus on this shimmering band of sun-gold.

3 After a few moments, allow the arch to vibrate gently, so that cascades of its sparkling golden crystals float gently towards you.

4 As they lightly touch your body, the crystals turn to golden dew drops that are absorbed into your skin.

5 Feel the internal warmth deep within you, as the golden hue surges through you, warming your body and soul and creating a wonderful glow.

6 Take a deep breath and, as you exhale, slowly open your eyes. Feel the way in which your mind and body have been recharged and revitalized.

For specific problems

 This flower meditation encourages you to think in images rather than words. It is designed to help you answer a specific question, or address a particular problem. The colour that emerges provides insight into your emotional state.

1 Find a comfortable place to rest and close your eyes.

2 In your mind, transport yourself to an exquisite garden, and sit on a grassy mound in the middle of it.

3 Flowers of every kind and colour surround you. Breathe in the heavenly fragrance while choosing a single bloom to contemplate.

4 Focus on the colour of the flower and think about a specific question you have in mind; ask for guidance while drinking in the colour's vibrations.

5 Allow your eyes to follow down the entire length of the green stem, into the roots and down into the earth below.

6 Take a deep breath and exhale. Now open your eyes. The colour of the chosen bloom is the key to solving your problem or dilemma. Let your intuition speak to you, and read the psychological profile of your chosen colour (see Colour Properties).

▼ IMAGINE THAT YOU ARE SURROUNDED BY AN ARRAY OF SWEETLY SCENTED FLOWERS.

For relaxing the mind

In Tibetan Buddhism, meditators visualize a teacher or an enlightened being, such as Buddha, and absorb his or her cosmic qualities using coloured light. This exercise helps to bring the energy of the mind into its natural, relaxed state.

1 Sit quietly for a few minutes. Think about all the teachers and spiritual beings who have inspired you with qualities of clarity, compassion and truth. Visualize their presence as a glorious light, suffused with translucent rainbow colours. Within the light, see a figure who represents all the wisdom in the universe.

2 From the forehead of the figure, a clear white beam of energy enters your forehead, filling your body with light and cleansing it of all negativity.

▲ FEEL THE CLEANSING ENERGY OF WHITE LIGHT ENTER YOUR FOREHEAD AND SPREAD THROUGHOUT YOUR BODY.

3 Now, from the figure's throat beams a ray of ruby-red light, which enters your own throat. This light fills your body and cleanses your senses of any negativity.

4 From the heart of the figure flows a ray of shimmering deep blue, which enters your heart and clears negativity from your mind.

5 Because you have now shared the purifying colour vibrations with this being of light, you have merged together so that now there is no difference between your energy and the clear, compassionate light of the universe.

▶ A REPRESENTATION OF THE SPIRITUAL GUIDE BUDDHA.

For personal development

Affirmations are a deceptively simple device that can be used by anyone, and they prove remarkably effective. Try using this method while in the meditative state, having previously planned and memorized the affirmations involved.

In using affirmations with meditation, you combine ease of communication with all parts of the mind and the effectiveness of repeated powerful phrases. The technique requires you to say to yourself, out loud, a positive statement about yourself as you wish to be. In order to make your affirmations effective, they should:

• be made in the present tense

• be positively phrased

• have an emotional reward.

If you notice what happens if you are asked not to think of elephants, you will realize why negatives (the words "no", "not", "never" and so on) have the opposite effect to that intended. Yours is the most influential voice in your life, because you believe it! Be aware of any negative statements that you make regularly about yourself, either to others or to yourself – "I am shy", "I am lacking in confidence", "I cannot", "I get easily nervous when . . ." and so on. These are all self-limiting beliefs that you reinforce each time they slip into your conversation or mind. Now you will be able to use affirmations whenever you are meditating in order to change those beliefs: "I am strong", "I am able to do this", "I feel really confident when . . ."

▲ AFFIRMATIONS CHANGE THE WAY YOU THINK ABOUT YOURSELF AND THE WAY YOU ACT AND REACT.

For peak performance

Visualization requires you to imagine yourself behaving, reacting and looking as you would wish to do in a given situation. This could be at an interview or a social gathering – any situation where peak performance is important to you.

In the same way that you can utilize your voice, so you can use your imagination. The imagination can stimulate emotions and can instil new attitudes in the mind. It can be a direct communication with your unconscious mind, and it can provide a powerful influence for improvements in your attitudes, behaviour patterns and overall confidence.

Imagine yourself at an important event. What will it mean for you? What will your reactions and those of people around you be? Most importantly, feel all the good feelings that will occur.

Imagination is like playing a video of the event in the mind's eye, from the beginning of the situation through to the perfect outcome. Get in touch with the feelings that will be there when you reach that outcome. Should any doubts or negative images creep into your "video", push them away and replace them with positive ones. Keep the scenario realistic, and base it upon real information from your past. Once you are happy with the images you are seeing, note the way you are standing and presenting yourself. Then allow yourself to view the scene from inside your imagined self. Now you can get in touch with the feelings and attitudes that will make the event successful. The best time to do this is when you are relaxed mentally and physically – during meditation. Teach yourself to expect new, positive outcomes. This can be combined with affirmations, to make the exercise doubly effective.

▶ REHEARSE THE FORTHCOMING EVENT IN YOUR MIND'S EYE SO THAT YOU ARE FULLY PREPARED.

For leaving troubles behind

This meditation, known as the "railway tunnel", is particularly helpful in leaving troubles behind, gaining perspective and focusing on the here and now. It can be very effective after the break-up of a relationship, loss of job or any major change.

Imagine yourself strolling along a straight flat path. It's a dull, cloudy, drizzly day. The path is leading between two high banks. There is damp grass beneath your feet, and you can see the cloudy sky above. You feel the weight of a heavy backpack on your shoulders, making your steps heavy and slow, and you seem to be looking at the ground in front of you as you trudge along the path, feeling damp and cold. You glance up and notice the entrance to an old railway tunnel: this must be a disused railway line. As you look, you can see a point of light at the other end of the tunnel, so it can't be too long. As you approach the entrance, the tunnel seems very dark, but that small circle of light at the far end is reassuring . . . At first it seems very dark, but the floor feels even and it is easy to walk along. As you do so, all those old doubts about yourself begin to surface; you are aware of your own failings, regrets and missed opportunities . . . Just

▲ IMAGINE YOURSELF ENTERING A DARK TUNNEL AND WALKING TOWARDS A CIRCLE OF LIGHT AT THE FAR END.

let them come gently to the surface of your mind. The backpack is getting a little lighter as these doubts and regrets surface, gently and easily . . .

You keep walking and notice a pool of light on the floor ahead . . . there must be an air shaft there. As you go through the pool of light, you suddenly remember a happy time, when someone really enjoyed your company . . . a time when you felt really good about being you. As you move into the darkness again, you feel lighter still; the backpack is emptying.

The circle of light at the end of the tunnel is growing, but here is another air shaft, with light penetrating the gloom. Again, as you pass through that light, another good memory of being appreciated for who you are, being praised or complimented, comes into your mind. Now you are back in the gloom, but it doesn't seem as intense as before. It is getting lighter and warmer with each step, and you experience more good memories of those who have loved you and happy events . . . As you near the end of the tunnel, you notice that the sun must be shining, and you feel so much lighter, as if you have lost that backpack altogether. A pleasant warmth begins to replace any traces of damp and cold that you felt before.

Eventually, you step out into the bright sunshine with a light tread, valuing yourself and the world much more. You realize you have so many opportunities awaiting you, and new chances to do things that make you feel good about yourself, building upon those positive events of the past. Your contribution is important – you are a valuable human being.

▼ WALK OUT OF THE TUNNEL INTO A BRIGHTER, LIGHTER WORLD.

For relaxation

Having trained yourself to meditate, you can utilize your "triggers" – evocative words and images – to take you back into a state of relaxation. If you have imagined a certain place, for example, doing so again will give you the same positive feelings.

It may be that you are aware of certain physical symptoms during meditation, such as a tingling sensation in the hands or feet: this may be a useful trigger, too. Imagine that you feel those symptoms, and within seconds you will gain the sensations and feelings associated with meditation. This can be especially useful before an important meeting, or any occasion about which you may be feeling a little apprehensive. Use the trigger to gain the calm confidence you need and to put things into their proper perspective. With practice, your mind will accept the training and linkages you have created during meditation, and will respond to these same signals at any time, quickly and easily, giving you instant access to all the benefits that come with deep relaxation.

▼ MEDITATION IS EXCELLENT FOR RECHARGING THE BATTERIES AND REDISCOVERING VITALITY, ENERGY AND WELLBEING.

For confidence in meetings

The meditative state, affirmations and visualization can all create a valuable preparation for a future event. Athletes use the power of these "rehearsal techniques" in training, and you can use them to achieve optimum performance in any situation.

- I am quietly confident in meetings.
- I speak slowly, quietly and confidently so that others listen.
- My contribution is wanted and valued by others.
- I enjoy meetings, as they bring forth new ideas and renew my enthusiasm.

Imagine a meeting that is about to happen, and see yourself there, filling in all the details that you know, and the people too; imagine yourself looking confident and relaxed, concentrating on what is happening. Be aware of the acute interest you have in what is happening – complete, concentrated attention – and then imagine yourself speaking: hear yourself speaking quietly, slowly and calmly . . . Notice people listening to what you are saying; they wish you well and support you, as you are expressing a viewpoint or raising a question they may well have wanted to raise themselves. Take notice of how you are sitting or standing, how you lean slightly

▲ IMAGINE YOURSELF AT AN IMPORTANT EVENT WHERE YOU FEEL AT EASE.

forward when speaking . . . that expression of calm confidence on your face. When this is clear in your mind, just like a film playing in your mind's eye, play it back and forth. When you are feeling comfortable with it, get into that imaginary you, "climb aboard" and be there in your mind, seeing things from that perspective. As you speak, get in touch with the attitudes that allow you to feel calm, in control, and quietly confident . . . It is like a rehearsal; the more you rehearse, the better your final performance will be.

For living for now

We cannot change the past, but we can learn from it and build up skills and useful insights from what we have experienced. The future is unknown – now is the only moment in which we can really make an impact.

◀ THE PAST IS OVER, AND YOU CANNOT BE SURE ABOUT THE FUTURE, SO THE ONLY TIME YOU CAN TRULY AFFECT IS NOW.

• I have learned from the past.
• The future is an exciting range of opportunities.
• I am able to enjoy my acute awareness of this moment.
• I am living NOW.
• I enjoy laying good foundations now on which to build a better future.

Imagine standing on a pathway that stretches in front of you and trails behind you, the way you have come . . . As you look around, you are aware that the area immediately around you – to the left, right and above – is brilliantly illuminated, and that sounds are amazingly clear. You are intensely aware of all that is happening around you, and your reactions to it. Look ahead again; you see the path in front, but it is dim in comparison with this area. As you check over your shoulder, you notice that the path behind is even less clear. A distant clock chimes, you take a step forward, and the bright, acute awareness travels with you . . . You notice the slightest of noises, movements or shifts of light, and take pleasure even in the sound of silence. You hear the same clock ticking, and with each tick take a small step forward, effortlessly, along the path . . . and illumination and awareness moves with you, in the here and now . . . At any fork in the path you can make decisions easily, because you are truly involved in the moment, rather than looking back at what might have been, or staring blindly into the future at what might happen. You enjoy an acute awareness of sound, hearing, feeling, taste and smell that is NOW.

For decision making

When a decision must be made, talking to an inner adviser can be helpful. Each of us has a higher self, made up of a conscience and an ideal self, towards which we strive. Meditation puts you in touch with your own inner wisdom.

First choose an adviser. You may wish to imagine sitting in front of a wise old person – someone you know, or an imaginary being. Some people choose to focus on an animal. Now imagine being with that adviser and asking a simple question about your problem, then wait . . . You may get a real insight straight away, or your adviser may use a symbolic present, or show you a scene to think about. They may even open up a possibility not yet considered. At first the answer may seem obscure, but at some

◀ DIFFERENT CULTURES HAVE ADOPTED PARTICULAR ANIMALS AS SYMBOLS OF WISDOM.

point the meaning will become obvious. We all have an inner adviser who is a source of wisdom – perhaps formed before birth, but who is constantly being brought up to date by our daily experience of the world and our reactions to it. The adviser is a valuable resource and can give you the confidence to make decisions, and move forward into your future.

▼ YOU MAY LIKE TO IMAGINE A FRIEND AS YOUR INNER ADVISER.

For improved health

The mind and body are so completely interlinked that if we keep physically fit, we will be mentally alert too. Likewise, if we utilize our mental capacities in a positive way, we can affect our physical health and performance for the better.

• I feel safe in the knowledge that my body is constantly renewing itself.
• It feels good to know that all damaged cells are replaced.
• My immune system is strong and fights off any infections easily.
• My mind and body are working in harmony to keep me healthy.

Imagine yourself lying or sitting comfortably. As you see yourself there, you notice a healing glow of coloured light surrounding your body, but not touching it. Let that colour become stronger, until it has a very clear, pure sheen, the colour of healing for you.

Now, as you watch, the healing light begins to flow into your crown. You can see it slowly draining into

▼ CONCENTRATE ON AREAS OF THE BODY THAT NEED HEALING, AND IMAGINE YOURSELF FREE OF ACHES, PAINS, ILLNESS AND TENSION.

◀ EXERCISE PROMOTES PHYSICAL FITNESS AND IMPROVES MENTAL CLARITY.

Now that the whole body is suffused with healing energy you notice the light concentrating in areas that need special attention. The warmth there seems more obvious as the light focuses upon repairing and replacing damaged tissue, and your own inner resources are focused in order to heal that area. Now you can allow the light to disperse again, and gradually return to your normal wakeful state.

all parts of the head, face and ears, starting its journey down through the neck and shoulders, into the tops of the arms . . . It continues to flow down through the arms and chest, the healing colour penetrating all the muscles and organs . . . as you watch, you can also feel a healing warmth coming into your body . . . NOW . . . as it flows down into the stomach, the back, all the way down to the base of the spine. At the same time, it is reaching your fingertips too, and that warmth is in your body right now . . . It continues to flow down through the legs towards the knees, down into the calves and shins, the ankles, the feet . . . all the way into the toes . . .

▼ A BALANCED AND NUTRITIOUS DIET IS ESSENTIAL TO GOOD HEALTH.

For reducing stress

Stress features in everyone's life, and can even be a major motivator in some circumstances. Meditation can be a great help in coping with stress. Combined with visualization, it can change your whole response to the demands of modern living.

• I enjoy solving problems.
• I keep things in perspective.
• I am a calm, methodical and efficient worker.
• I love the feeling of having achieved so much in a day.
• I enjoy being calm when others around me are not.

Imagine yourself in a situation that has in the past caused stress. Picture the situation, and the other people involved . . . See yourself there . . . and notice a slight shimmer of light between yourself and those other people . . . a sort of bubble around you . . . a protective bubble that reflects any negative feelings back to them . . . leaving you able to get on with your tasks . . . your life, with an inner strength and calmness that surprises even you. The protective, invisible bubble surrounds you at all times. It will only allow those -

▼ YOUR PROTECTIVE BUBBLE WILL STAY WITH YOU ALWAYS, WHATEVER YOU DO.

feelings that are positive and helpful to you to pass through for you to enjoy and build upon. Others may catch stress from each other . . . negativity, too, can be infectious . . . but you are protected . . . you continue to keep things in perspective . . . and to deal with things calmly and methodically. You are able to see the way forward clearly . . . solve problems . . . find ways around difficulties . . . by using your own inner resources and strengths, born of experience.

Now see yourself talking to someone who has been causing tension in your life. Find yourself telling them that what they are doing is unhelpful in resolving the problem or difficulty. Find yourself able to let them know in such a way that they can accept this without offence . . . and find your own calmness and control . . . a strength that supports you. You can let someone know if too much is being expected, and explain why. See yourself in that situation . . . calmly explaining the areas of difficulty . . . being able to supply examples and information until they understand the position. Ask them to prioritize – or give new ways

▲ TRY NOT TO LET WORRY DISTORT OR MAGNIFY YOUR PROBLEMS AND DIFFICULTIES.

that things can be dealt with. At all times you are surrounded by that protective bubble of light that keeps you calm and quietly confident. Next, imagine pushing out through that same protective bubble emotions that are unhelpful . . . past resentments . . . hurts . . . and embarrassments. Push them out through the bubble . . . where they can no longer limit or harm you. You are now better able to control the way you feel and react . . . The bubble stays with you and enables you to remain in control . . . keeping things in perspective . . . having the strength to change those things you can change . . . accept those things that you cannot . . . and move on.

For concentration

The pressures that are experienced when studying for an exam or learning a new skill can disrupt concentration, and so one's ability to absorb information. A visual image used during meditation can help re-energize your ability to learn.

• I enjoy moments of insight and understanding.
• I enjoy using my mind and expanding the boundaries of my knowledge.
• My memory forms links between the known and the new information.
• My learning ability improves with use.
• I concentrate so completely that nothing but an emergency can distract me.

Imagine a huge jigsaw puzzle spread out in front of you: it is a giant picture made up of many smaller images, and each image is a jigsaw puzzle in itself. Some images are nearly complete, others are only just starting to form, some even seem a confused jumble of unattached pieces. Focus your attention on one image, one part of the giant puzzle that is nearly complete but is still a little confusing.

A new piece comes into your hand and it fills a gap as it interlocks with all the surrounding pieces . . . The image suddenly becomes clear, and you can see it now. You have a wonderful feeling of achievement: that which was confusing is now fully understood. You feel as you do when a new piece of information interlocks with others and you understand the whole subject. This insight . . . the joy of understanding . . . is what makes learning so worthwhile.

Should you ever need to retrieve that piece of the puzzle, to answer a question of some kind, you know that all the interlocking pieces will arrive with it to give insight and understanding – you can select and use them as you wish. The memory is like a giant puzzle, and the moments of achievement when understanding and enlightenment occur are the joy of learning itself and an important part of life's beauty.

As you learn, so you enjoy total concentration as you study and gain information. Only an emergency could distract you. Learning is a continuous part of being alive.

For achieving goals

In all areas of life – personal relationships, social interactions and career – having a goal is important in focusing your attention and inner resources. A goal provides a sense of direction, and ultimately brings the joy of achievement.

Be aware of the different areas of your life: work, social, emotional and spiritual. Select one for this exercise . . . think about what you want to achieve and describe your goal on paper before beginning.

While in the meditative state, imagine that you have achieved this goal. Surround yourself with the things or people that indicate that you have achieved the goal. Be as specific as you can . . . be aware of all you see, hear, touch or sense . . . Be there . . . make it real . . . be specific about colours . . . temperatures . . . lighting. Be there and know how it feels to have achieved that goal . . . how it affects your mood.

Now, from where you are at that moment of achieving that goal . . . look back . . . as though along a pathway of time . . . to where you were . . . and notice the stages of change . . . of movement towards achieving the goal . . . the actions

you have taken . . . the contacts that you have made . . . the people involved. Be aware of the smallest moments of change that have occurred, from the start of the journey to its fulfilment . . . Remain in touch with the feelings that will make it all worthwhile . . . feel more determined to take one step at a time . . . make just one change at a time . . . Become more determined to be successful in the achievement of your goal . . . Take the first step towards it, today.

▶ VISUALIZE YOURSELF TAKING ONE STEP
AT A TIME TOWARDS YOUR GOAL.

For increased creativity

Many adults long to be creative but underestimate their ability to be so. Self-expression takes many forms, and everyone is creative in one way or another. Use these exercises to discover your latent talents and build confidence.

- I enjoy my own creativity.
- I am blessed with having a vivid imagination.
- I love to express myself in creative ways.
- I enjoy my own imaginative responses to the world as I see, feel and experience it.

▼ As children we are all naturally creative and this creativity remains with us into adulthood. It is there within us just waiting to be rekindled.

Imagine yourself in a wonderful room . . . a room surrounded by windows looking out on to countryside . . . In this room there are many small areas, and you can move freely around trying each of the areas to see how you feel . . . Here on the left is a large piece of paper with pens and pencils, in a small studio for drawing and sketching . . . Another area has an easel and paints set out for you, the artist, to take up . . . Another has clay for you to handle and form into shapes or pots . . . Another has a computer ready for you to create images in poetry or prose . . . Yet another has engineering tools for the inventor . . . Here is one with cameras and photographic equipment . . . Just spend a little time moving around and trying them all . . . these are some of the areas into which you may choose to channel your own creativity, and where no one else need judge or approve. Only your opinion matters, and the joy of translating the inner

▶ THERE ARE SO MANY DIFFERENT WAYS TO EXPRESS ONE'S CREATIVITY.

world of the imagination into a form or expression that suits you . . . Which feels most stimulating, most exciting, most comfortable?

Become aware that everyone has a creative ability – to tell stories, to create beauty, to capture a moment . . . Imagine yourself using one of the areas in this marvellous room, or finding another area not yet described . . . in order to create your response to the world around you, or your inner world. Be aware of the feeling of having time and energy to channel into this creative activity . . . the ability to utilize your innate creativity . . . and the joy that comes when something tangible forms in front of you.

Sometimes we drive smoothly and happily along a road, we come to traffic lights on red and have to pause. The creative flow can be like

that too, but the lights turn to amber and then green and off we go, just as you will when a temporary block dissolves . . . Enjoy your creative and imaginative power, and translate it into the world around you. You can do it, for your own sake . . . free of the need to please anyone else but yourself.

▼ INSPIRATION CAN COME IN MANY DIFFERENT FORMS: NATURAL OR ARTIFICIAL; REAL OR IMAGINARY.

Index